Muskrat and Mink

Trapping with Pap

DENNIS H. KELLER

Illustrated by C. W. Houghtaling

PAGE PUBLISHING
Conneaut Lake, PA

First originally published by Page Publishing 2023

ISBN 979-8-88793-407-5 (pbk)
ISBN 979-8-88793-417-4 (digital)

Printed in the United States of America

Introduction

The American Indians learned the art of trapping long before the early settlers came to North America. The Indians valued the warmth as well as the beauty of the furs they obtained. Trapping since then has provided a source of income for those who have participated in this sport. Trapping also has helped wildlife managers control certain animal populations through established regulations.

The purpose of this book is to instill interest, knowledge, and love for the sport of trapping. It provides a good foundation on what equipment is needed if one is going to pursue this sport. It also explains how to properly prepare your trapping equipment. It gives the reader some background knowledge about muskrats and mink and what types of sets are commonly used to catch muskrats and mink. Information is also given on how to skin, flesh, stretch, and dry your pelts.

Since many children do not have fathers, it shows how a grandfather can have a positive influence on his grandson. Having read this book, the reader will have increased knowledge on the art of trapping, will experience trapping success, and will develop a love for the sport.

It was the end of September and the time of year to clean up the garden and place all the tomato stakes, garden equipment, and tools in the shed. It was a cool, brisk morning here in central Pennsylvania, so Pap Keller wanted to make sure all his yard and garden work was completed before cold weather arrived.

Pap's grandson, Lance, would often come and help his pap with some of the chores. This Saturday morning was no different. Lance lived a short distance down the narrow country road with his mother, so it was an easy and a short bike ride to his pap's house.

Lance had a special incentive to come and help Pap this morning. He knew his gram was planning on baking caramel rolls this morning and was hoping they were out of the oven long enough for him to get a taste. As he opened the outside kitchen door, he could smell the aroma coming from the freshly baked rolls on top of the stove. Pap was just finishing his cereal and ready to have a caramel roll with his hot cup of coffee.

"Have one of Gram's warm caramel rolls, Lance. There is some juice and milk in the fridge. Grab a glass out of the cupboard and help yourself," invited Pap.

"You don't have to invite me twice for one of Gram's delicious caramel rolls," said Lance as he opened the refrigerator door to get some milk.

"Hey, Lance, I could use some help down at the garden. I need to clean up my garden and put a few things back into my shed," suggested Pap.

"Sure, Pap, I'd be glad to help with that task," said Lance. "Let's go do it."

So after they finished eating, they both headed down to the garden area at the lower end of the yard.

"Lance, why don't you pull out those tomato stakes and carry them over to my shed," Pap suggested.

Lance was glad to do just that along with a couple other chores his pap wanted him to do this morning. While stacking the tomato stakes in the corner of the shed, Lance couldn't help but notice the steel traps hanging from the rafters. "What did you use these traps for, Pap?" asked Lance.

"Well, I use to trap muskrats, mink, raccoon, and fox in my younger days. I've been saving these traps along with some other trapping supplies and thinking I might get back into this sport again. I really enjoyed trapping, and the money I earned helped me to buy a few other sporting items," Pap informed Lance. He knew by the look in Lance's eyes that he may be interested in knowing and learning more about trapping.

"Well, Lance, let me give you a little history about trapping. Trapping is one of the oldest occupations of men. The Indians used trapping to provide food and warm clothing for themselves and their families. They made all kinds of things from the animals they trapped. Steel traps, like you see hanging here in the shed, have been used since the early 1800s.

"You might be interested in reading about a man named Sewell Newhouse. He made steel traps as well as guns in his blacksmith shop. He was also friends with the Indians in central New York. The Indians marveled at the guns and traps Newhouse made in his shop. Soon Newhouse began selling his traps to hardware firms and to people interested in making money trapping wild animals.

"Anyway, Lance, I just thought you might be interested in how trapping got started," Pap said as he sat down on the nearby bench.

"Have a seat, Lance, we'll take a short break," Pap suggested as he gave out a deep breath.

Pap continued talking and suggested that Lance read about Daniel Boone and Christopher (Kit) Carson.

"Why would you want me to read about Daniel Boone and Kit Carson?" asked Lance.

"Well, Kit Carson and Daniel Boone were trappers. Daniel Boone spent his winters trapping and was known as a master backwoodsman. He fought with the Indians, and his wilderness adventures are legend. Kit Carson, on the other hand, was a successful trapper and served as a guide on expeditions throughout the Rocky Mountains. He was an Indian fighter as well. As a matter of fact, he married a Comanche Indian girl which is quite interesting. If you want to learn more about these men, look them up in your school's library and see what else you can learn or find out about these men," suggested Pap.

Lance responded jokingly, "I don't want to fight any Indians, Pap, but I wouldn't mind learning more about trapping. Perhaps you could teach me how to trap, Pap."

"Well, I know you would get a lot of satisfaction being outdoors and communing with nature while trapping," remarked Pap. "Plus, trapping helps our state wildlife agency control and manage our wildlife populations. Remember that muskrat we saw swimming along the stream bank when we were trout fishing last spring?" asked Pap.

"I sure do. He was an active little creature. I bet he was gathering food for his family," Lance answered.

"Well, Lance, muskrats are one of the easiest animals to catch. So if you are interested in learning how to trap, I could teach you. Trapping muskrat would be a good place to start," remarked Pap.

"We might even get lucky and catch a mink which are more difficult to fool and catch. It is going to take some preparation and time scouting our local streams to find fresh muskrat or mink signs such as feed beds, dung piles, slides where muskrats enter and leave the water, and underwater den entrances. Trapping season in our state doesn't begin until November, so we have time to prepare if you are interested in learning this sport," added Pap.

"Why do we have to wait until November to trap?" asked Lance.

Pap then informed Lance that the fur of the animal you are trapping must be "prime."

"What do you mean by prime, Pap?" asked Lance.

"It is when the animal's fur is of superior quality. Cold weather helps the fur to become thicker. You never want to kill a fur bearer until their fur is prime. Since muskrats don't hibernate, they are still very much active during cold weather," Pap answered.

"Wow, that is interesting! How did the muskrat get its name?" asked Lance as he was now getting more interested in what his pap had to say.

"Well, it gets its name from the musky odor produced by a pair of scent glands found under the skin on a muskrat's belly between the hind legs," informed Pap.

"What do you do with the muskrat's hide?" asked Lance.

"Manufacturing companies make collars, coats, and other garments using muskrat and mink fur. The fur of the mink and muskrat is soft and thick. Their underfur is tight and covered with guard hairs which make their fur shine. Garments made from this fur can be rather expensive and are prized by women," Pap added.

"What do you think, Lance? If you are interested in learning how to trap, I would be willing to teach you what I know from experience and what I have learned from other trappers," said Pap.

"I sure would like to give it a try," answered Lance.

"I have traps and some stretchers. We will have to purchase some other trapping supplies. We will need a roll of number 14 gauge wire, some lure, name tags, hip boots, a couple sharp skinning knives, and so on. Since my traps are rusty, we will need to boil them in a special solution. I can show you how I boil my traps to remove any rust or foreign odors. Let's take a walk someday along Big Fishing Creek and see if we can find muskrat or mink sign. I know most of the landowners, and I'm sure they will give us permission to trap where the stream flows through their property.

"If you are free some night after school or on some weekend, we can go on a scouting mission. Muskrats can have as many as two litters annually, so hopefully, we will find where they have been active," Pap suggested.

"Tomorrow is Sunday. I know you and your mom go to church in the morning. Are you free in the afternoon, say, around two?" asked Pap.

"I think so. I'll have all my school homework done. Can you pick me up in your truck?" asked Lance.

"I sure can. We better put on our waders in case we need to enter the water to check out visible sign or if we have to make a creek crossing," Pap responded.

Lance and his pap finished with the chores, and Lance departed for home. He was anxious to tell his mother what he and his pap were going to do the next day. The next afternoon could not come soon enough for Lance. As planned, Pap picked up Lance at his house. "Do you have your hip boots?" asked Pap.

"Sure do. I hope they don't have any small holes in them. A leaky boot can give you a cold, wet foot," Lance laughed as he threw his boots in the back of the truck.

Lance hopped in his pap's truck, and they traveled short distance to a parking spot along Big Fishing Creek.

They put on their boots and headed for the water's edge. As they were walking along the stream bank, Pap pointed out what looked like some muskrat paths through the tall grass and leading to the creek's bank.

"Look, Lance. This is where some muskrats are leaving and entering the water. This is a muskrat slide, and this is where we will want to set a trap," Pap informed Lance.

Pap then pointed out some underwater den holes in the stream bank. "We can place a trap just inside each hole or place a body hold trap on the outside of each hole. Muskrats sometime build houses or lodges, too. I don't see any here, however," Pap said as he continued to show Lance the various muskrat sign.

Pap then showed Lance a feed bed where some roots, water plants, and grass were piled up. "We can place a trap in the middle of that feed bed and camouflage it with some of the feed bed material. I think that would be a sure catch. Now I am starting to get excited after seeing all this sign," exclaimed Pap.

Pap and Lance continued walking along the creek's edge. Soon they came to a steep bank along the water's edge. "If the water is not too deep along this bank, we could place a blind set here," suggested Pap.

"Lance, do you see the dung piles on that large rock? These dung piles look moist which is a sign the muskrats are visiting this place on a regular basis. We could make a blind set along this bank and even make a cubbyhole or pocket set with bait near here. I usually cut an apple in quarters and place a piece on a sharpened stick back in the hole and about five to six inches over the pan of the trap. You could bait your trap with a carrot or parsnip as well if you so desire. Adding a few drops of commercial muskrat gland lure would be helpful. The muskrats would have to cross over the trap to get to the bait and lure. I'll send for some muskrat and mink lure this week. That way, we will have it in time for trapping season," Pap informed Lance.

After spending several hours scouting and picking out some locations to set their traps, they headed back to the truck. "Lance, by the looks of things, I think we have a good chance to catch a few of these muskrats. We may even get lucky and catch a mink. Let's head home and see if Gram has any snacks for us. I'm getting a bit hungry. If my memory serves me well, I think Gram baked some chocolate chip cookies early this morning," said Pap as he held his stomach.

"I'll second that motion, Pap," said Lance.

They then hiked it back to Pap's truck, took off their hip boots and placed them in the back of the truck, put on their shoes, and headed home.

"Hey, Pap, my socks are still dry. I must not have any holes in my boots," Lance said with a smile.

Lance and Pap soon arrived back at the house where they consumed quite a few delicious cookies. Gram said, "Now don't spoil your supper. I'm preparing a roast beef meal. Lance, your mother is joining us for supper."

Pap and Lance laughed as they gulped down their last bite of cookie.

"Well, Lance, we have some preparations to do before trapping season," Pap said.

"What's that Pap?" asked Lance.

"We have to boil our traps and make some name tags as required by law and securely fasten a tag with your name and address to each trap. Did you see that woven wood pack basket hanging in the shed?" asked Pap.

"Yes. I wondered what you used that for," answered Lance.

"Well, that's my old trapping basket. We'll use that basket to carry some of our equipment and any muskrats we happen to catch," said Pap.

"Let's pick out a day and time to boil our traps. Since my traps are very rusty, I'll soak them for a day or two in 1:3 white vinegar to water to help remove a lot of the rust. I have a large plastic tub I can use. Afterward, I will power wash the traps to get them ready to dye. Some trappers boil their traps in a mixture of water, lye, and hardwood ashes. I think it is easier to use vinegar. I will do this sometime this week, Lance, so the traps are ready when you come to help dye the traps. We can fix up an area in the garden for our fire. I have a large metal container to hold the water. After the water begins to boil, I can add some walnut hulls to help dye our traps. I also have some logwood trap dye to add to our boiling water. This boiling process will remove any rust or foreign odors from our traps. We should put a galvanized roofing nail between the jaws of each trap. This will permit the dye to coat the trap jaws on the inside and give our traps a nice black color. After our traps are boiled, we'll hang them out to dry," Pap continued to inform Lance as to what preparations they would have to make.

"What do you say we meet next Saturday morning and get this job behind us? I'll lay up some old cement blocks to make a firepit. I have wood stacked behind the shed for our fire. I'll gather up some old walnut hulls underneath my walnut tree."

"Sounds good. Next Saturday is free for me, so let's plan on it!" Lance responded enthusiastically.

"Okay then. I'll get the fire started early and gather what we need to accomplish the task. Let's meet at 9:00 a.m.," suggested Pap.

"Okay with me. Let's do it," Lance responded enthusiastically.

Soon Lance's mother arrived for supper, and together, they enjoyed eating Gram's roast beef dinner. After helping with the dirty dishes left from supper, Lance and his mother headed out the kitchen door.

"I'll see you next Saturday morning, Pap," shouted Lance.

"Love you, Pap. Love you, Gram!" Lance and his mother shouted as they departed.

The next Saturday morning, Lance rode his bicycle to his Gram and Pap's house. Pap already had the fire started in the garden. Pap had laid all the traps out on the ground next to the fire.

"Good morning, Lance. Did you get a good night sleep?" Pap asked.

"Yes! Matter of fact, I got to bed earlier than usual because I knew we had some work to do this morning. I see you have everything ready, Pap," remarked Lance.

"Yes, I even took time this week to adjust the pan levels on each trap so they are level with the top of the open trap jaws, and I filed some of the triggers and receivers to eliminate any round edges. I also stamped out some copper name tags for you this past week and securely fastened a tag with copper wire to each trap," Pap said.

He then grabbed one of the traps and showed how the pan level was adjusted just right.

"Wow, you've been busy, Pap. Those trap name tags look neatly done. I sure thank you for doing all this preparation to help me get started," said Lance.

"Why, that's what paps are for!" exclaimed Pap.

"Now let me show you how to set a trap without getting your fingers caught in the jaws," Pap said as he picked up a trap and held it on his knee.

"You press down the trap spring(s) to open the jaws of the trap—placing the trap trigger under the pan receiver. Next, hold the trap in one hand and use your thumb on the other hand and put it under the jaws of the trap. Now press down on the trap pan with your thumb to get a hair trigger," instructed Pap.

Pap then snapped the trap with his thumb and handed it to Lance. "Now, Lance, you try it," instructed Pap.

Lance struggled at first. Finally, he soon got the hang of it.

Pap then had Lance set a conibear trap. "Conibear was the name of the man who invented this body gripping trap. This trap may be a little more difficult for you to set. However, if you are standing in creek water, you will need to use your knee or thigh to set your traps," Pap emphasized.

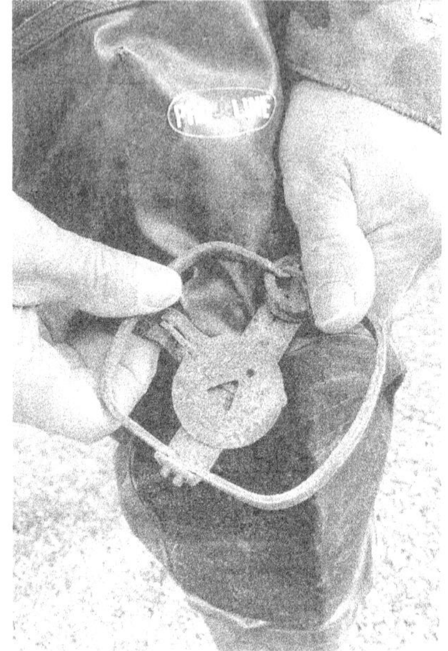

Pap had various kinds and sizes of traps laying on the ground that he wanted to boil. Pap pointed out some of the old Victor jump traps in his collection. "They don't make these jump traps anymore. I liked them because they were a light compact trap and easy to bed in the stream. I sure caught a lot of muskrats with these old jump traps," Pap said.

"What is this trap with the extra-long wire spring?" asked Lance.

"This is a stop loss trap. Some trappers call it a guarded foothold trap. After the muskrat is caught, that long spring is released and flies up against the upper part of the leg. This helps to keep the animal from twisting or wringing off its foot, which is caught by the trap jaws, and then escaping," informed Pap.

"Does the muskrat die if it loses its foot?" Lance asked.

"No, they don't bleed to death. I remember catching muskrats with just three feet. It is best, however, if you can make drowning sets or use conibear traps so this does not happen," Pap explained.

Pap further explained, "You need to rig your traps in such a way that the animal will drown as soon as possible. A muskrat or mink's natural instinct is to head for deeper water once caught. The weight of the trap will pull the animal's nose under the water for the animal to humanely drown. Your grandfather, Arthur W. Keller from Lock Haven, Pennsylvania, came up with a technique to facilitate this using what I call the Keller Drowner, named after my father's last name.

"You cut about a four- to five-foot straight limb with plenty of side branches. You cut off the side branches to about a half inch—just long enough so the trap's chain ring can slide over the top. You want to keep your branches at the end of the limb long enough to stop the ring. The half inch cut branches prevent the animal from swimming back to shore and thus drowning. When you make your set, slide the ring over the largest end of the limb and push the limb into the stream bank. Your Keller Drowner is perpendicular to the stream bank. We can make some of these drowners ahead of time using our hunting knives.”

“What a neat invention, Pap. Your dad sure knew what he was doing. Sounds like an old Indian technique,” remarked Lance.

“Well, my dad claimed he was part Indian, so maybe it was an old Indian technique.”

“Another way to fasten your trap chain is using twelve- or fourteen-gauge wire and securing your trap chain to a large anchor rock. You then place this rock further out in the stream. Usually, a foot of water is enough to drown a muskrat or a mink. I’ll demonstrate this for you when the time comes,” said Pap.

“Wow, Pap, I’ve learned a lot already,” remarked Lance.

“I’m happy you feel that way. Actually, you will learn a lot more through experience just as I did during my early days of trapping,” said Pap.

Before long, the water in the metal large-mouth container began to boil.

“I gathered some walnut hulls containing tannic acid and placed them in the water. I found some logwood dye to add to the water as well,” Pap told Lance.

Pap used a large stick to churn the water. Pap then wired a few traps together by their chain rings and dropped them into the boiling water.

"We'll let these traps simmer in the water for about an hour or more," explained Pap.

"The longer you boil these traps, the darker the traps will become. This process will help the traps resist rusting. While these traps are boiling, let's take a break and go up to my house and get a snack. Gram made some corn pone cake this morning. It will taste good with milk and sugar," Pap suggested with a smile.

"Oh, I love Gram's corn pone! Let's go get some!" Lance said enthusiastically.

After enjoying a couple dishes of corn pone, Pap and Lance ventured back to the garden area to check their traps.

"Let's pull these traps out of the water, Lance, and hang them on the tree limb near my shed," Pap suggested. "We could let our traps soak overnight, but I think they look just fine. We sure don't want the rust showing. These black traps will have a more natural color."

Finally, Lance and Pap got all the traps boiled and hung out to air-dry.

"Let's remove our metal tub and supporting rods and let the fire die down. We will then add some damp green vegetation to the hot embers to make smoke. Fetch my old woven wood pack basket and we will hang it, along with some of our other equipment, over the smoke. This will help eliminate any foreign or human odors that may contaminate our equipment," suggested Pap. "Another step trappers used for added trap protection is to boil their traps in an odorless trap wax to seal the logwood dye treatment. We'll save this step for another time."

"I think we have enough traps to get you started. We have a good variety of traps suited for different locations. We have a pack basket, some wire, a pair of cutting pliers, our hunting knives for making bait sticks, and our hip boots. We can buy some rubber gloves, but I just usually use my bare hands. The water can get pretty cold on the hands and forearms however. A lot depends on the outside temperature too. Oh yes. We can add a garden trowel to our basket to help us dig holes or level our trap beds. Sometimes, I just use the soles and heels of my hip boots to level an area," Pap said.

"Do we need a license to trap in Pennsylvania?" asked Lance.

"Well, since you are under twelve years of age, you won't need a license, especially since I will be mentoring you. Because you are turning age twelve next year, you will need to complete the required Hunter-Trapper Education Course. Then you can apply for a junior license," informed Pap.

"I'm looking forward to taking that course next spring, Pap, and obtaining a training certificate so I can apply for a license," replied Lance.

"Oh, I think you will have a lot of fun taking this course. Plus, you will learn a lot," said Pap.

"I'll have to dig out my senior license. It is in the bottom of my gun cabinet where I keep my ammunition, turkey calls, and other hunting paraphernalia," Pap remarked.

"Trapping this year begins on November 19th and ends on January 8th…and there is no limit on the number of muskrats you can catch. What we should do now is get an idea as to where we want to make our sets. We can make a few Keller Drowners and decide what style of trap we want to use at each set location," suggested Pap.

"Let's do it, Pap!" Lance shouted.

"Okay then, we could do this some evening after school or some weekend morning. The muskrats should be pretty active gathering food, making feed beds, slides, and digging den holes in preparation for winter," Pap added.

Soon it was the beginning of November, and Lance and his pap finished their scouting the area streams again for mink and muskrat sign and picking out several set locations.

Pap said," Sometimes you have to use your boot to poke around the bank to find den holes that are hidden from the naked eye. You don't always see a muddy trail leading in and out of the den."

They also made some Keller Drowners in preparation for the upcoming season and placed them near where they were going to be used. They picked out some large rocks to which they would wire and fasten their trap chains as well.

In the meantime, Lance practiced setting traps on his knee and thigh so he can better assist his pap when making the various sets.

Pap admitted, "I might be a bit rusty, but I have not forgotten many of the methods and techniques I utilized when trapping in my younger days. I'm anxious to show you what I have learned so you can become an experienced and knowledgeable trapper."

By the looks of all the muskrat sign that we were lucky to find when scouting ahead of time, our success is almost guaranteed. Once we catch some muskrats, I will demonstrate for you how to skin, flesh, and dry our hides. Pelt care should take place soon after the muskrats are dispatched. Since a muskrat's fur will probably be wet, we should hang them up in an airy place where the fur can dry before skinning them. If we handle our pelts in the correct way, we will get top value for them. Once we skin and flesh our muskrat hides, we will need to stretch the hides. I'll show you how to do this. I have some wire and wooden stretchers hanging in my shed. They will give our hides the desired form," Pap emphasized.

"Well, Pap, it looks like I have a lot to learn. I'm glad I have a good teacher," remarked Lance.

"Thank you, Lance. I think we are going to have a great experience. I'm enjoying showing you what I know about this interesting sport," Pap said.

Soon Lance headed home to tell his mother what he and Pap had planned. She was excited and happy that Lance and his pap were going to spend some quality time together. She also knew that Lance would like trapping since he had a general interest in the outdoors and what it had to offer.

The first day of trapping season arrived. After having a good breakfast, Pap loaded their trapping gear on to the back of his pickup truck. He then drove to Lance's house where he was anxiously waiting. It was almost 7:00 a.m. when they headed to Big Fishing Creek where they planned to begin their trapline. Pap parked his truck not too far from the creek. They slipped on their waders, picked out a few supplies, placed them in the pack basket, and headed for the creek's edge.

It was a brisk and clear morning and perfect weather for trapping. The two waded into the water and began making sets. Pap demonstrated for Lance how to properly place the traps at the various set locations. He showed Lance how to conceal the traps placed in feed beds and at slide locations using shredded grass and leaves. They also made cubbyhole and pocket sets.

They then baited the traps with apple quarters impaled on a sharpened stick and placed five to six inches above the trap pan. Pap reminded Lance that their bait should not be visible from the air because it could attract a bird or hawk. Where appropriate, they added some commercial muskrat and mink lure. Body gripping traps were used in front of the underwater burrows leading to den holes in the bank. They placed large enough sticks to snugly fit through the holes in the conibear springs to stabilize these traps.

Where possible, they slipped the trap ring on Keller Drowners and pushed the drowners into the stream bank and just beneath the water if possible. In some cases, Pap and Lance used wire fastened to the trap ring and to a large rock placed further out in the stream where the muskrat could drown. They occasionally would use a stop loss trap so the muskrat, when caught, would not be able to twist or wring off its caught foot. They also made a couple blind sets with hopes of catching a muskrat or mink traveling along the stream bank, a bridge peer, or beneath some tree roots hanging over the stream's bank.

Pap told Lance that he liked to place the traps so the trap jaws face down stream. He also emphasized bedding their traps so they don't wobble. He explained that muskrats and mink will work their way up stream while feeding or hunting and then travel the water current when they head downstream. They added some mink lure at some of these locations with hopes of getting a mink to cross over their trap that was firmly placed in the streambed and camouflaged with natural vegetation. Pap also told Lance that mink like fresh bait. They are not attracted to spoiled meat.

After a few hours, Lance and his pap completed their trapline. Needless to say, they were a bit tired.

"I can't wait to get these hip boots off," said Lance.

"Me too! Let's head back to my house to rest and have a good healthy lunch!" exclaimed Pap.

They loaded their leftover gear into the truck bed and headed home.

While eating their lunch, Pap told Lance that they should check their trapline that evening.

"Let's go out around 10:00 p.m. and see if we have had any luck. I always liked to check my traps on the first one or two nights. Often, you will catch two muskrats at the same set during the first one or two nights," Pap suggested.

"That's fine with me! I can hardly wait!" Lance exclaimed.

So they just did what Pap suggested. Sure enough, they caught four muskrats on their first check. Lance held the flashlight as Pap removed the drowned muskrats and reset the traps.

The next morning, Pap and Lance headed to Big Fishing Creek at daybreak to check their trapline again. Pap informed Lance that the law requires trappers to check their traps at least every thirty-six hours.

"Personally, I like to check them sooner than that," said Pap.

Wouldn't you know it, Pap and Lance scored a "double" in a couple of their traps—meaning they caught two muskrats in the same trap in one night. Pap had Lance remove some of the caught muskrats and then reset the traps. They put the 'rats' in the basket and moved on, checking the rest of the sets. Yes, it was a successful first day of trapping; and after a couple hours, they had completed checking their trapline—removing the caught muskrats and remaking sets. Pap and Lance caught eight muskrats the first morning. They now have a total of twelve muskrats to skin soon after their fur dries.

"We didn't catch any mink, but we sure did well catching muskrats. I remember the first time I caught a mink. I caught it at a muskrat den entrance. That mink was probably looking for a muskrat to kill and eat. If I remember correctly, I received twenty dollars for the mink from the local fur dealer," recounted Pap.

"Boy, I hope I catch a mink someday. That would be exciting. I know they are smart and can be hard to catch in a trap," said Lance.

"Well, we did make a couple mink sets, so maybe a mink will make a wrong move and step into one of our traps," encouraged Pap.

Pap and Lance then headed home and hung their muskrats in Pap's shed so the fur could dry. The muskrats were hung by the front feet to dry.

"You shouldn't hang them by their tail because any moisture will penetrate into the fur. The fur should be brushed free of mud or any other debris as well. We don't want to wait too long before skinning and fleshing these rats to prevent spoilage or pelt deterioration. We will then have to put them on our stretchers. I will make sure my skinning knife is sharp," said Pap.

After a couple nights had gone by, Lance and his pap had several muskrats to skin.

"We'll use the *case* method. We can sit on this wooden bench. It will be easier on our backs," said Pap.

Pap, using his trusty, old but sharp skinning knife, demonstrated for Lance how to skin a muskrat. After making the initial cuts, he showed Lance how he pulled the hide over the carcass.

"Just like pulling off your sweater," laughed Pap.

He used his knife only when necessary when removing the hide.

"Now you have to be careful when cutting around the ears, eyes, and mouth," Pap emphasized as he made each cut. "This takes a little skill as well as practice," Pap said as he completely removed the hide on the first muskrat. "Now you try it, Lance, with your skinning knife," encouraged Pap.

Pap assisted Lance as he removed the skin on the second muskrat. He naturally had some difficulty removing the skin around the eyes, ears, and mouth.

"The more muskrats you skin, the better you will get," encouraged Pap.

It took some time, but Pap and Lance finally completed skinning all the muskrats. Pap emphasized the importance of keeping their skinning knife sharp and suggested using a good "wet stone" for this purpose. Next, they pulled the hides (flesh side out) over wooden stretching boards to facilitate the fleshing process. Starting with the head and working towards the tail, they carefully removed the surface fat and flesh from the hides. Pap and Lance used a kitchen knife and large spoon in the fleshing process. Removing all the fat and flesh is important to prevent spoilage.

Next, the hides (fur in) were pulled snug over the wire stretchers and secured with the hooks that come with the wire stretchers. They made sure the pelts were centered on the stretchers—eye and ear holes on one side and front legs and belly on the other side. Pap and Lance were careful not to stretch the hide too much and risk ripping the hide. Pap also told Lance that overstretching the hide would make it less dense, thus causing them to get a lower value. Pap also emphasized that you never want to use salt on your muskrat hides when preserving them. Soon all the hides were put on stretchers and hung in Pap's shed to dry and out of reach of any mice. The shed was dark and well ventilated. Pap told Lance that the temperature in the shed should be kept around fifty-five to sixty degrees Fahrenheit if possible. They made sure the pelts did not touch one another. This would cause spoilage where they touch.

"Who will buy our furs, Pap?" Lance asked.

"The Pennsylvania Trappers Association, Inc. will have a list of buyers. We'll check with them. You might want to join this organization. I know they have a rendezvous every year. That would be fun for us to attend that event."

"Let's do it, Pap!" exclaimed Lance.

"Okay. I'll find out the date, and maybe we can attend," said Pap.

During the next couple weeks, Pap and Lance would get up early in the morning before school and check their trapline. On Tuesday night, during the second week, the weather got really cold. Lance told his pap that they probably wouldn't catch anything due to the cold weather.

"Well, we still have to check our trapline. You will never know unless you check your traps. Besides, it is the law," reminded Pap.

So on Wednesday morning, Pap got up extra early, heated up his truck, scraped the frost off his truck's windows, and headed to Lance's house. They could see their breath in the air as they tramped along their trapline.

"It sure is pretty snippy out this morning," said Lance.

They were not having any luck until they reached the last leg of their trip. Then, as they approached the blind trap set made underneath tree roots sticking out onto the water, they saw a drowned animal in their trap that didn't look like a muskrat from a distance.

"What is that in our trap?" Lance asked.

"Well, let me pull it up out of the water and see. I hope it's not what I call a water rat!" exclaimed Pap.

As Pap pulled the long slender animal with short legs and a long tail out of the water, he could see that it was a large brown mink.

"I think we caught one. I think we caught our first mink, Lance," Pap said with excitement in his voice.

Sure enough, it was a large male mink. Pap took the mink out of the trap and handed it to Lance.

"Wow, Pap, I never saw a mink up this close. Its fur is nice and thick. I'm so excited! I never thought we would catch a mink this year. This catch sure makes my year!" Lance exclaimed as he put the mink in their pack basket. "Let' hurry home and show Mom and Gram," suggested Lance.

After checking the few sets left, they headed home with smiles on their faces. It was evident that they were pleased with themselves.

"I'll have to find a stretcher for our mink, Lance. If I can't find one, I'll make one. I have some one-quarter-inch thick white pine boards we can use to make a wooden stretcher. When we skin out this mink, we need to skin out the legs, but keep the feet attached to the pelt. As for the tail of the mink, we will have to take our knife and open the underside of the tail," instructed Pap.

Pap and Lance trapped muskrat and mink for a couple more weeks. They were catching fewer muskrats, so Pap suggested that they pull their traps and hang them in the shed for another year.

"Lance, we better save some muskrat for next year. It is not a good practice to catch every last muskrat," advised Pap.

Soon the hides hanging in the shed were dry and ready to be sold. Pap and Lance removed the hides from the stretchers and prepared them for shipping. They used a shipping tag provided by a licensed fur dealer that Pap had chosen to buy their furs. The completed tag listed the number of muskrats and mink being sent.

"We have quality furs, so we should get a good price for them," remarked Pap.

Before long, a check arrived in the mail for Lance. Of course, Pap insisted that Lance keep and use the money for more trapping supplies or something else.

Pap said, "My payment was the satisfaction of teaching you how to trap and seeing the look on your face when you caught that large brown mink."

Lance thanked his pap for introducing him to the sport of trapping muskrat and mink. Both were looking forward to spending time along the trapline again next year.

Lance H. Keller

Trapping Supply List

body gripping (conibear) traps—#110

coil spring foothold traps—#1 1/2

long spring traps

roll of #14 gauge wire

pliers

muskrat and mink lure

trap tags with your name and address

waterproof trapping gloves—eighteen inches

hip boots/waders

wire and/or wooden stretchers

fletching tools—butter knife, spoon

sharp skinning knife and sharpening stone

bait—apples, fish, etc.

catchpole to restrain and release animals

flashlight for checking traps at night

trapping license

Keller Drowner

To make a drowner, cut a four-to-five-foot-long branch with a lot of side branches from a shrub. Cut off the side branches leaving about a half inch protruding from the main branch. Then slide the trap ring over the drowner and push it into the stream bank. When the muskrat or fur animal is caught in the trap, he most likely will head for deeper water. The cut off branches catch the ring of the trap, thus preventing the animal from returning to the stream bank. The weight of the trap pulls the animal down in the water causing it to drown. Keep enough long branches at the end of the drowner to keep the ring of trap from sliding off.

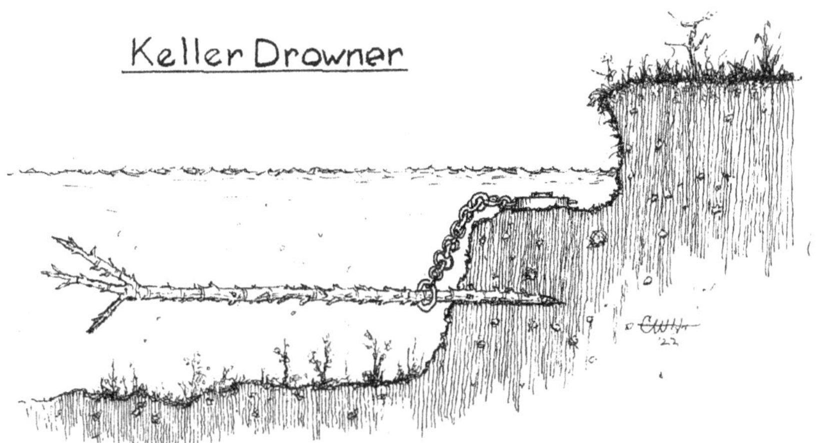
Keller Drowner

The Musky Muskrat

The muskrat (ondatra zibethicus) is actually a rodent native to North America, is semi-aquatic, and lives near still or slow-moving water. It gets its name from the strong-smelling odor that comes from a substance called musk released by two perinea glands the size of lima beans located between the muskrat's thighs. This musky smell is used to mark their territory. Muskrats are eighteen to thirty-six inches in length and weigh up to four pounds. They actually look like a small beaver.

The muskrat is primarily a vegetarian but will also eat small animals such as crayfish, frogs, and fish. They make holes in stream banks that are usually underwater. Their tunnels lead to nesting chambers under the ground. They also make houses made of mud and plant material with underwater entrances. Muskrats are very prolific in that they can have up to five litters per year. The females produce milk to feed their babies. Muskrats do not hibernate. They are excellent swimmers and are strong fighters if attacked by a mink or other creature. They are most active at night or near dawn or dusk.

Muskrats have a unique scaly and flattened eight- to twelve-inch tail with no hair. Their tail is used as a rudder when swimming and helps them to propel through the water. It is also used as a prop when standing on its hind legs. Their hind feet are partly webbed that helps them when swimming. The muskrat can swim underwater for up to seventeen minutes. Their underfur is dense, silky, and soft and are covered with long dark brown glistening guard hairs. This hair protects them from the cold water.

The muskrat is one of the favorite animals to trap. They are easy to catch, and their hides are valued. They are used by garment industries for collars, coats, etc.

The Elusive Mink

Mink (mustelidae) are semi-aquatic carnivorous mammals that are native to the Northern Hemisphere. They have long slender bodies with pointed snouts and weigh up to two pounds. They have short legs but can cover an area up to three miles in diameter. Mink make their homes in hollow logs, stone piles, under large tree roots, abandoned muskrat dens, etc.

Mink have a lust for killing like that of the weasel. They have excellent eyesight, hearing, and their good sense of smell becomes advantageous when searching for food.

The mink are vicious and will attack mostly anything. They kill their prey by biting them on the back of the head or neck. They prefer fresh food and will prey on mice, fish, crayfish, amphibians, birds, muskrats, etc. Mink are agile, fierce fighters, and excellent swimmers. Their feet are partially webbed.

The mink have a deep, chocolate brown fur that is thick and soft. They also can be black. Their underfur is covered with long guard hairs that help to make the pelt shine. They also have a long six- to eight-inch bushy tail. One thing that distinguishes the mink is the small white patch of fur on its chin. They are valued for their luxurious fur. Their hides bring good prices, so they are highly prized by trappers. Mink are smart and hard to catch even for the experienced trapper.

If using bait to catch mink, it needs to be fresh such as a piece of muskrat or fish. Adding lure to your set is also helpful. Since mink like to travel along bridge abutments, run on logs, go through culverts, and travel under exposed tree routes, these would be good places to set a trap.

SLIDE SET

FEED BED SET

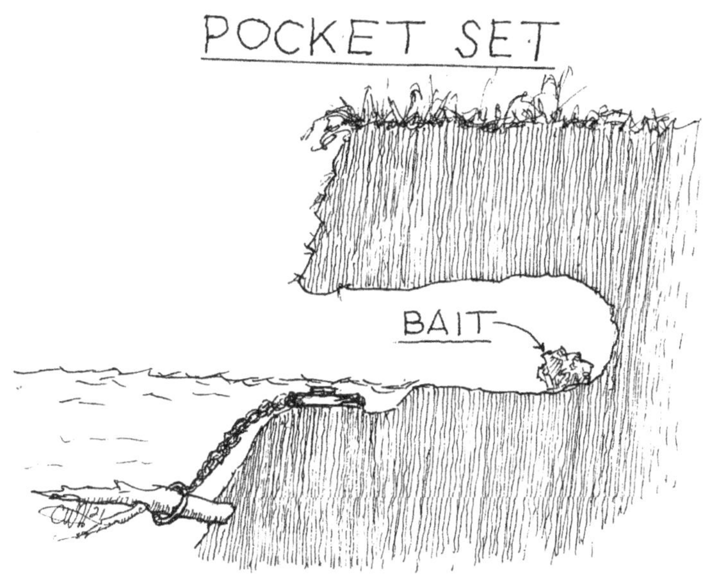
POCKET SET
BAIT

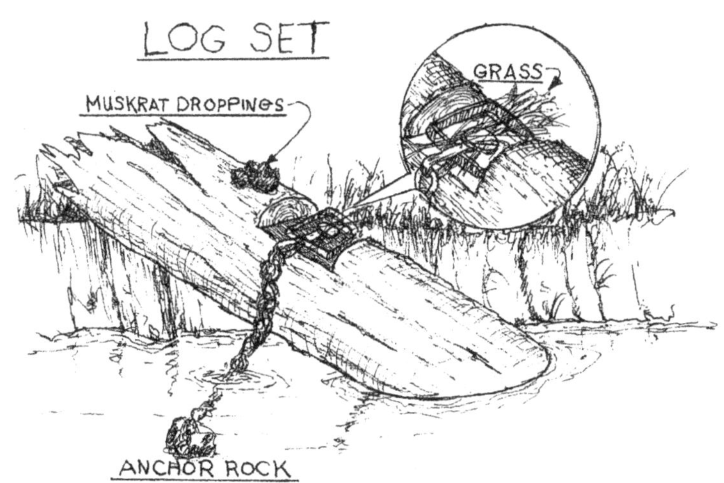
LOG SET
MUSKRAT DROPPINGS
GRASS
ANCHOR ROCK

BLIND SET
ANCHOR ROCK

BRIDGE BLIND SET
ROCK ANCHOR

CUBBY SET

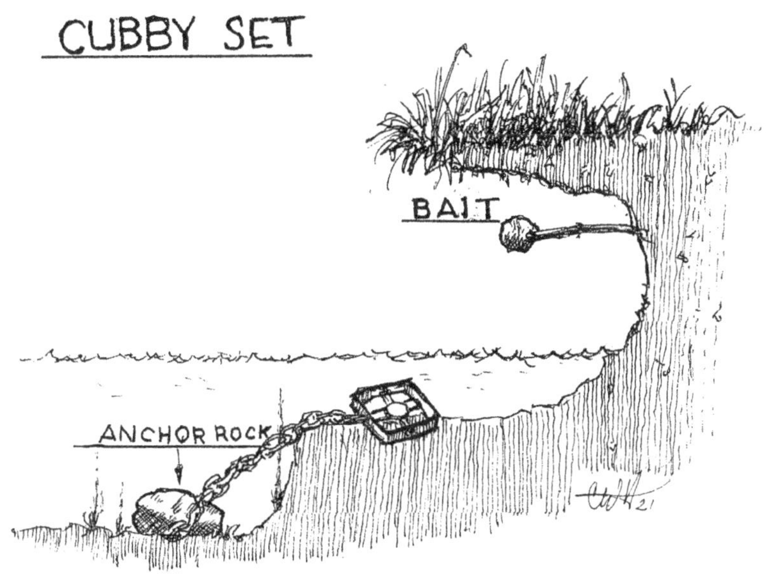

ROCK SET

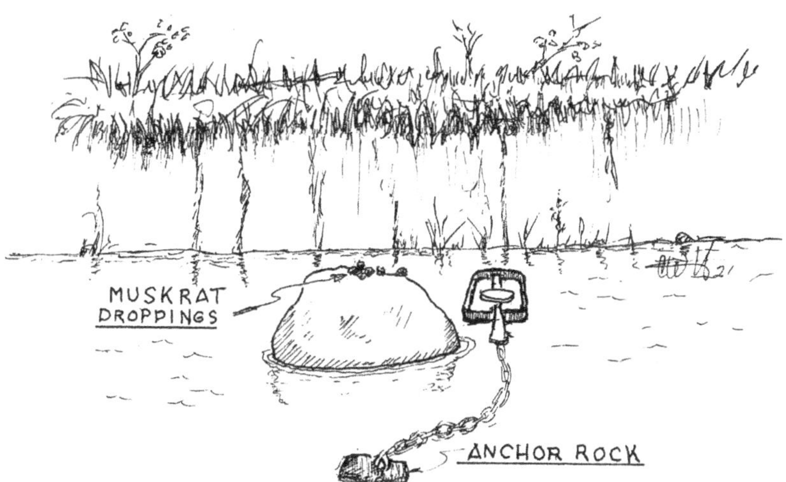

ANCHOR
ROCK
DEN HOLE SET

UNDER WATER ENTRANCE SET
DEN
CONIBEAR TRAP

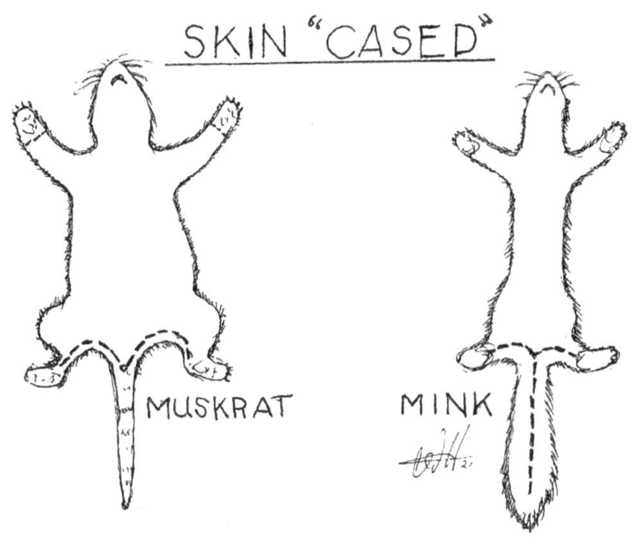

SKIN "CASED"
MUSKRAT
MINK

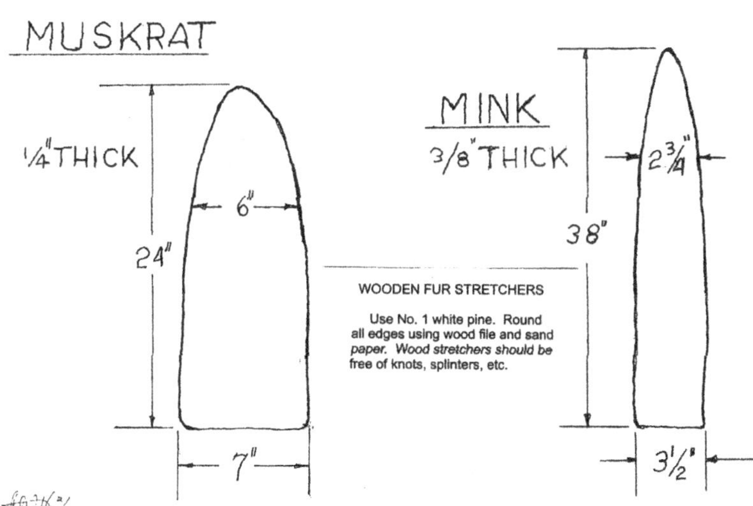

MUSKRAT
1/4" THICK
6"
24"
7"
MINK
3/8" THICK
2 3/4"
38"
3 1/2"
WOODEN FUR STRETCHERS
Use No. 1 white pine. Round
all edges using wood file and sand
paper. Wood stretchers should be
free of knots, splinters, etc.

Old Shipping Tag

FROM

Name

Street

City

State

Zip Code

PLACE POSTAGE HERE

To

GEO. I. FOX CORP.

RAW FURS

115 WEST 30TH STREET
NEW YORK, N.Y. 10001

TEAR OFF ALONG THIS LINE

INSIDE STUB

**PRINT YOUR NAME AND ADDRESS
AND PLACE INSIDE BUNDLE**

Name

Street

City

State   Zip Code

FOR **GEO. I. FOX C**ORP.

115 West 30th St., NEW YORK, N.Y. 10001
(212)-564-4127

SHIPPING INSTRUCTIONS

1. Print your name and address on this tag and attach this part to outside of package.
2. Fill out attached Stub and place inside package.
3. Always ship furs by parcel post if possible.
4. Avoid using heavy boxes as it increases Express Charges. Packages and boxes must be securely nailed, sewed, wrapped or tied. Write or call for more tags if needed.

IMPORTANT - PARCEL POST PACKAGES MUST NOT CONTAIN ANY OTHER WRITING THAN NAME, ADDRESS AND CONTENTS. SEND INSTRUCTIONS IN SEPARATE ENVELOPE.

Mark on List below the Number of Skins in Shipment

Mink	Lynx	
Raccoon	Marten	
Skunk	Coyote	
Muskrat	Badger	
Opossum		
Otter		
Red Fox		Lbs. Wild Ginseng
Grey Fox		Lbs. Cult. Ginseng
Beaver		

FILL OUT AND PLACE INSIDE BUNDLE

Check Skins Carefully Indicate on Stub Amount You Ship. Our Count Must be Accepted as Correct.

Mink	Lynx	
Raccoon	Marten	
Skunk	Coyote	
Muskrat	Badger	
Opossum		
Otter		
Red Fox		Lbs. Wild Ginseng
Grey Fox		Lbs. Cult. Ginseng
Beaver		

Gram's Recipes

Gram's Corn Pone

Ingredients:

3/4 cup sugar

1 and 1/2 cup of flour

1 egg

3/4 cup of shortening

1 cup of sweet milk

1/2 teaspoon of baking soda

1 teaspoon of baking powder

1 cup of corn meal

Procedure:

Mix together and bake 350 degrees for thirty-five to forty minutes.

Gram's Caramel Rolls

Ingredients:

2 loaves frozen bread
3/4 cup oleo
1 and 1/2 cup brown sugar
2 small vanilla pudding mix—cooking type
4 tablespoons of milk
cinnamon to taste
nuts/raisins

Procedure:

Thaw dough. Do not let rise. Break one loaf in pieces (about a size of walnut and put in buttered 9x12 pan). Melt oleo. Add sugar, dry pudding, milk, and cinnamon. Mix well and pour over dough in pan. Break up second loaf and put on top of sauce. Let rise about 2 and 1/2 hours. Bake at 350 degrees for thirty minutes.

Bibliography

Carman, Russ. *From Trapline to Fur Shed (3rd Edition)*. Pennsylvania Trappers Association, Inc.

Failor, Paul L. *Pennsylvania Trapping and Predator Control Methods*. Harrisburg, Pennsylvania Game Commission, 1974.

Fergus, Chuck. "Minks and Muskrats," *Wildlife Notes*. Harrisburg: Pennsylvania Game Commission.

McCracken, Harold and Harry Van Cleve. *Trapping*. New York: A.S. Barnes and Company, 1967.

About the Author

Dennis H. Keller, the author, grew up in the small town of Salona, located near Big Fishing Creek in central Pennsylvania. He participated in various sports, but the one sport that he particularly liked was that of trapping. His father, Arthur W. Keller, introduced him and his brother, Arthur W. Keller II, to the art of trapping at a young age, and they both fell in love with the sport.

For starters, they purchased some jump and long spring traps plus other trapping equipment. They practiced setting traps on their knees. Their dad then helped them boil their traps in wood ashes and walnut hauls to remove any oils and to give them color. Their dad also showed them the different sets to make along the stream's edge in order to catch muskrat, mink, and coon.

At first, they took their muskrats to the local fur dealer who gave them cash for their catch. Later, their dad taught Dennis and his brother how to skin, flesh, and stretch the muskrats they caught. They made wooden stretchers at first and then later bought wire stretchers. Then, at the end of the season, Dennis and his brother carefully packed up their hides and sent them to a fur company that evaluated their hides and then sent them a check.

As they became older and perfected the art of trapping, Dennis and his brother ran their own trapline. They scouted for good trapping spots and checked their traps each morning before school. In the evening, after doing their homework, Dennis and his brother would head to the basement to skin out and flesh the muskrats they caught that morning, and then they would put them on stretchers.

After completing high school and college, Dennis became a teacher and later, an elementary school principal. His brother worked as a math teacher for a couple years and then worked for the Department of Defense. To this day, they both cherish the days they spent on the trapline thanks to their father.

Dennis had also written and published a book entitled *Whitetail Deer Facts and Strategies*. It is a complete guide with a wealth of information for hunting deer.